Teaching the Craft of Writing

Revising & Editing

by Kathleen Hurni-Dove

New York • Toronto • London • Auckland • Sydney
Mexico City • New Delhi • Hong Kong • Buenos Aires

Teaching *Resources*

Dedication

For young writers everywhere

Acknowledgments

Tedra Hemingway at J.R. Watson Elementary School

The students at DeKalb Central United School District

The students from Fort Wayne Community Schools

Thank you to my husband and family for your unconditional love
and support!

Thank you to Lola Schaefer for encouraging me as a writer.

Thank you to Joanna for your patience.

✳ ✳ ✳

Cover Design by Maria Lilja
Cover Illustration by Kristen Balouch
Interior Design by Sarah Morrow

Copyright © 2006 by Kathleen Hurni-Dove
All rights reserved.
Published by Scholastic Inc.
Printed in the U.S.A.
ISBN 0-439-44403-9

1 2 3 4 5 6 7 8 9 10 40 11 10 09 08 07 06

Table of Contents

Introduction

For the past twenty years, teaching students to write has been a personal journey. As a teacher, I've watched myself transition from story starters to writing formulas, to class bookmaking, until I arrived at writing workshop, which is truly the most powerful approach I've experienced. When I established my first community of writers, I knew a workshop that allowed students the opportunity to create their own authentic writing pieces was the best choice for teaching students to write. Writing workshop provides differentiation. Every young writer works at his or her own pace within the writing cycle. During workshop time, I see drafting, revising, conferring—most importantly, I see writers who care deeply about each other's writing.

As a writing consultant and facilitator, I assist teachers with implementing a workshop format in their classrooms. As a first step, I help teachers create a safe classroom environment where the teacher and students work side by side in a community rich with print, language, and literature. Within this community, we offer students modeling, demonstration, and lots and lots of practice. Next, we teach our students to become a receptive audience for each other. As part of an audience, young writers not only learn to listen and talk like writers, but also they develop a respect for each other's work.

A writing workshop has many advantages; it

- encourages a love of writing
- develops independence and responsibility
- allows students the opportunity to discover their own writing process
- provides students with life-long tools
- teaches students to think and envision possibilities
- differentiates learning
- creates an appreciation and understanding of both craft and genre
- fosters respect for writing and each other

I believe students become better writers when they are provided daily opportunities to write during a workshop. Choice of topic encourages ownership. Studying genre and immersing students with quality literature helps students learn the writing craft. Most importantly, students discover their own process. Through thinking, planning, and practice, they learn how they work as writers. With our encouragement and support in a workshop, young writers will develop a lifelong love of writing.

Chapter 1

What Is Revision?

An Introduction and Kickoff Lesson

Years ago when I was teaching kindergarten, I remember a small group of boys and girls building with wooden blocks. It was center time in our classroom and the students decided to build the White House. Now, this was during the era that George Bush senior was President of the United States. The students had built many rooms in the house, including a red room, a blue room, and a green room. Their enthusiasm bubbled as sharing time approached. Suddenly, one little girl reminded the others that President Bush had grandchildren. She said they needed to build a schoolroom and a playground at the White House. If those important rooms were not added, then the grandchildren wouldn't have a place to learn and play while visiting their grandparents. I watched carefully as the students enthusiastically added, removed, and rearranged blocks creating two new rooms for the Bush grandchildren. That morning I marveled at the students' thinking. It was awesome. They were kindergartners working cooperatively while demonstrating great thinking skills. They were smiling. They were having fun. Little did I know that the students were practicing a critical part of the writing process: revision.

Years later, while teaching second grade, I attended a staff development reading/writing workshop presented by Lucy Calkins. In the beginning of her presentation she asked, "What is your curriculum for play?" She reminded the audience that talk and play were the foundation of language arts. Immediately, I thought of the kindergartners who had built the White House. In their play they added blocks to create a playground and a schoolroom to better fulfill their purpose—creating a White House for a president with grandchildren. That is the heart of revision, and that morning was a golden moment for me as a writing teacher. I realized that revision is play. And play is fun! I knew from that time on, I needed to approach the teaching of revision as the playful part of writing. But I first needed to adjust my own attitude toward revision.

For years I had wanted to write for children. I enrolled in courses, attended workshops, and purchased a children's book market guide. I had family, writing peers, and even published authors critique my work. Each one of them asked questions, made suggestions, and offered sound advice.

What did I do with all this information? Just what students tend to do—I put my writing pieces back in my writing folder and let them sit. The prospect of revision was daunting.

I gave up, thinking I wasn't a good writer. If only I knew then what I know now, I could have published many of my pieces. I was neglecting the most important part of the writing process, missing an opportunity to play with language, to experiment, to make my good ideas even better. I thought of revising as work, and the need to revise as personal rejection. I feared my students felt the same way. The idea of revision as play revolutionized my teaching—and my writing life as well!

I began thinking of my own writing as a puzzle. Puzzles are both fun and challenging. I kept moving, deleting, and adding until all the pieces fit. When helping students to revise, I started approaching revision the same way, designing lessons that encouraged creativity, exploration, and thinking. This approach gives students the opportunity to see their own writing sparkle if they spend time playing with words and phrases, moving parts around, and rewriting the same piece for a different audience.

In the following pages, I will share ideas and strategies that will help students understand the revision process and approach it with a positive, playful attitude. I'll share examples of lessons that you can teach in your own classrooms. I've tested each of the strategies suggested in this book in my own classroom with my own students as well as with students in classrooms all over the country as part of my staff development work. Some may work well for you. Others may not. If something falls flat or doesn't seem right for your students, simply revise it to make it fit. And don't forget—HAVE FUN!!!

Revision Through Play

To engage second, third, and fourth graders in playful revision, use this hands-on activity. It works with materials such as straws, Legos, pattern blocks, clay, or toothpicks.

1. Give each student materials. Allow them a short period of time to create a building, design, or figure.

2. Next, have them take something away from their creation.

3. Then, have them add something.

4. Ask students to move parts. Talk about the effects their changes—their revisions—had on their original creation.

5. Now invite them to turn the same materials into something new.

Take this lesson one step further with students by brainstorming outcomes of adding, deleting, moving, or transforming. Apply this to real-life situations such as cooking or construction. The possibilities are limitless.

What Exactly Is Revision?

Revision is changing writing to make its meaning clearer. Writers need to ask themselves

- *Who is my audience?*
- *What is my purpose?*

Once writers have answered these basic questions, they can reread their writing to ensure it makes sense for their particular audience and purpose. Writers may ask

- Does my writing make sense?
- Does my writing sound right?
- Will my writing keep my readers interested?
- Have I provided enough details and examples?

- Is the writing organized in a way that makes sense?
- Do my words create pictures?

Notice that all of these questions focus on the content, organization, and development of the piece. Revising is about making meaning clear. Too often students confuse revising with editing. Editing deals with the mechanics of writing, such as spelling, punctuation, paragraphing, and grammar. These are important matters, and I will discuss editing in Chapter 5. But as I introduce revision, I am careful to keep the focus on meaning—making the writing clear for the audience, making sure it says just what I want.

The Kickoff Lesson: Using Poetry to Introduce Revision

Penning a poem with the class during shared writing is one of my favorite ways to introduce revision. I discovered this while I worked as a writing mentor at an elementary school. The classroom teacher asked for support with a genre study of poetry. As a result of her own school experience, she feared poetry. Before I came in to model, I asked her to spend two weeks immersing her students in all forms of poetry by reading aloud poems whenever she had the opportunity. For example, during math she read poems about adding, subtracting, and fractions. During history she read poems about the states, famous people, and our country. And during science she read poems about insects, electricity, and machines. In addition, students were asked to read poems independently. Each student was provided an index card and was encouraged to tally each poem read independently. The goal for each student was to read 50 poems before my visit. The excitement for this project sparked interest throughout the school. It wasn't long before the principal posted poetry outside her office for students to read, the cooks hung poems in the cafeteria, and the custodian wrote his own poetry and shared it with the students.

By the time I arrived, her students knew that some poems rhyme and some don't; that a poem can be about anything; that poems come in all shapes and sizes; and that some poems repeat words, phrases, or sentences.

On my first afternoon with them, I guided the students to draft list poems. We started by writing a class poem during a shared writing lesson. It was wintertime, and a snowman outside the classroom window seemed like the perfect topic. Since it was shared writing, I chose the topic and guided students through the writing. The students generated the words and I recorded them, prompting students to expand their descriptions and asking questions to elicit more information. Students could easily experiment with language and sound since I was responsible for the action of writing. This is an effective way to demonstrate the power of revision. The lesson went something like this.

Mrs. H-D: I noticed someone built a snowman outside the window.

Micah: Some kids in my sister's class built it at recess.

Mrs. H-D: I think we should write a poem about the snowman.

Micah: Could we give it to my sister and her friends?

Mrs. H-D: What an excellent idea! We now have an audience. (*I write* snowman *at the top of the chart paper.*) Let's go over and look out the window. Take a minute and look at all the snowman's features. What are some things you notice?

Nik: He has a hat.

Mrs. H-D: Describe his hat. Be specific. Try to paint a picture with your words.

Nik: An old red hat.

Mrs. H-D: Who else notices something about the snowman?

Madison: He has sticks for arms.

Ryan: He's starting to melt.

Kate: He's smiling.

Ryan: No he's not. He's crying because he's melting.

After a few more comments, we return to our seats on the floor and I ask the students for five nouns that make them think of the snowman. The students decided on the following five words: *snowball, scarf, arms, hat,* and *snow.* I jot them on the chart.

Mrs. H-D: Tell me what kind of snowball.

Paul: Round snowball.

Mrs. H-D: Tell me more. I need to see the snowball in my mind.

Sean: I know. Three snowballs round as the moon.

Mrs. H-D: Say something about the size of the snowballs.

Sean: One small, one medium, one big.

Mrs. H-D: Let's read what we have so far. (*I read the poem aloud.*)

> *Three snowballs round as the moon*
> *One small, one medium, one big*

Mrs. H-D: Sounds good so far. Tell me about the hat.

Nik: An old red hat covers his head. No. An old red hat warms his head.

Mrs. H-D: I like the sound of *warms his head.* (*I record the lines on the chart paper.*)

Sean: When we looked outside at the snowman, Ryan noticed he was melting. I think we should say the sun warms the old red hat.

Mrs. H-D: Good thinking. How can we describe the scarf?

Adele: Since he is melting, let's say that his knotted scarf drips.

Sydney: And his stick arms droop.

Mrs. H-D: Very nice. These words show the snowman is melting. Let's reread. (*The class reads the poem together.*)

> *Three snowballs round as the moon*
> *One small, one medium, one big*
> *The sun warms the old red hat*
> *His knotted scarf drips*
> *His stick arms droop*

Mrs. H-D: Say something about the snow.

Daniel: Melting snow.

Mrs. H-D: What does the melting snow do?

> *My experience has been that even young writers will give time and effort to revision if the audience and purpose are important to them.*
>
> — Regie Routman (2000)

Nik: I know. I know. It turns the snowman's smile upside down.

Mrs. H-D: Wow. Look at what we've done. We started with five simple words. We added words, deleted words, and moved words around. These changes make our meaning clearer. Writers, this is revising. Let's read the poem aloud. As you are reading, think about how the words sound.

> Three snowballs as round as the moon
> One small, one medium, one big
> The sun warms his old red hat
> His knotted scarf drips
> His stick arms droop
> Melting snow
> Turns
> The
> Snowman's
> Smile
> Upside
> Down

Sydney: Since the snowman is melting, I think we should change the second line so the audience knows the snowman is melting.

Mrs. H-D: How could we do that?

Sydney: I think the second line should say *one big, one small, one smaller*.

We returned to this piece many times until most of the students were satisfied. From their study of poetry, several students remembered that many poems feature a repeating line. Since Ryan mentioned the snowman crying, the students decided to repeat the word *crying* three times at the end. As you can see, the poem went through many revisions. When the piece was completed, the class presented it to Micah's sister and her friends. The final version looked like this.

> The Melting Snowman
> Snowballs as round as the moon
> One big, one small, one smaller
> The spring sun warms his old red hat
> His knotted scarf drips
> His stick arms droop
> Melting snow
> Turns

Sharing Time

In my classroom, at the end of each writing workshop, three students share. A writer sits in the author's chair and shares their piece of writing. I encourage the students to establish a purpose for the share. For instance, a student may ask the audience to listen for how their piece sounds, or if the writing makes sense, or if they used strong vocabulary. The audience's responsibility is to listen, give three appreciations for what the author did well as a writer, and then ask three questions that will help the writer's writing. I record the questions on sticky notes and hand them to the student writer at the end of the share. The notes serve as reminders and encourage revision.

The
Snowman's
Smile
Upside
Down
Crying
Crying
Crying

Mrs. H-D: Writers, you've done a nice job of revising. You've played with the words by adding, changing, and moving them around. When writers spend time playing with their words, they are revising. Revising helps our readers to understand our writing because it is clear, has purpose, and flows.

Composing poetry through a shared writing lesson is a powerful format for the teaching of revision. As soon as the students orally started adding, deleting, and moving words and phrases, they experienced the revision process. Knowing they had an audience who would truly appreciate their poem, the students were willing to invest their time as a simple list transformed itself into the image of a snowman, filled with emotion, as he slowly loses his life to the fading season.

This experience drove home the importance of audience and purpose. I realized that all students, especially older ones, need an audience and a purpose to make revision meaningful. If no one is going to read the writing, what's the point of trying to make it clearer?

Student Portrait: Chase Revises an ABC Book for Kindergartners

Right before school was out I had a second grader, Chase, who wrote an ABC book. While conferencing, I noticed his piece was an alphabet list. I asked him who his audience was going to be. He told me he was writing this book for the kindergarten class and as soon as it was published he was taking it down to his former kindergarten teacher's class to read. I smiled when he said his book would teach the kids their ABCs. I asked him to share his work with the class.

After he shared his piece, the class found three sound appreciations for the things he had done well. Adele said she appreciated his idea to make an ABC book for the kindergarten class. Madison commented on the fact that he kept his focus while he was writing. Brandon told Chase he appreciated the time he spent before writing thinking about his audience. When it was time for questions/suggestions, Sam raised his hand. He suggested that Chase add alliteration to his piece to make it stronger. Chase thanked Sam for his suggestion. The next day Chase revised his piece. *A is for apple* became *A is for Anna's apple, B is for butterfly* became *B is for beautiful butterfly*, and so on; see an excerpt of his work on the next page. Revision was important to him. He knew from the beginning who his audience was going to be. Because he had a purpose, he was open to suggestions about his writing and eagerly tried out the alliteration to make his ABC book even better for those kindergartners.

The lesson is this chapter introduces students to revision as an exciting part of the writing process, a time when they can play with language to make meaning clearer. In the next chapter, we'll look at some specific strategies students can try when they want to achieve a particular goal in their writing.

A is for apple

B is for butterfly

C is for cactus

D is for dinosaur

E is for electricity

F is for flower

G is for goat

Chapter 1 Review

- Think of and introduce revision as a form of play.
- Revision is the process of making meaning clearer.
- If students know their audience, they take the time to revise.
- Poetry is a great way to introduce students to revision in writing.

Chapter 2

Revision Strategies That Enrich Writing

Once students understand the purpose of revision and have experienced the playful approach to making writing clear, I begin to teach specific revision strategies. I tell students that revision is revisiting writing, and revisiting requires rereading. Students reread during the kickoff lesson, but now I explicitly draw their attention to this first step in revision. I do this by modeling how I revise my own writing. I put my stories on the overhead, revisiting them many times. Each time I revisit a piece of writing, I rewrite, thinking aloud about how I can make it clearer for my readers.

As helpful and necessary as rereading is, student writers need explicit instruction on what to listen for and how to actually revise their writing. In this chapter, I share a series of mini-lessons I use to teach basic revision strategies.

Organizing for Revision Instruction

As I describe in the introduction, my students keep a writing notebook. When I begin formal revision instruction, I have students dedicate one tabbed section to revision. Here they record the strategies I teach and take notes on the lessons. This section becomes a resource students use as they revise, helping them build a repertoire of strategies.

The format of my revision lessons is consistent.

1. Introduce the strategy; students write it in their notebooks.

2. Explain why and when writers use it.

3. Model how to use it on a piece of writing.

4. Invite students to apply the strategy on their own work.

This format is helpful to me as I plan lessons and it lets students know what to expect.

Determining which lesson to teach when requires careful observation of your students and consideration of your teaching goals. There are three main ways I select lessons.

1. ***Conferences.*** When I confer with students, I take anecdotal notes. Periodically, I review the notes and see what instructional needs emerge from the group.

For instance, if your records indicate overuse of adjectives, you may want to teach a revision lesson on deleting extra descriptive words.

2. ***Responses to Writing Prompts.*** If you are required by your district to administer and score writing prompts, you can use this assessment to inform your instruction. During scoring, you may notice weak beginnings and endings. Then you will teach specific revision lessons on leads and endings. Ask students to practice the strategy by returning to their work and rewriting, making sure to explain to students that when they revisit their work, they are revising.

3. ***State Standards.*** Many schools require certain standards to be taught each quarter. You can use these standards to guide your instruction.

Revision Strategy Lessons

The following is a list of possible problems you may notice in students' writing. Following each problem is a mini-lesson that teaches a revision strategy. I present these lessons on large white chart paper, an easel, or the overhead, and students record them in their notebook.

> **Problem** ✳ ***Students are not varying sentence beginnings or sentence structure.***
>
> **Strategy** ✳ **Rewrite sentences.**

Mrs. H-D: One thing that writers do is to vary their sentence beginnings. Writing can sound boring when every sentence starts the same way, and we don't want our audience to get bored! Please choose a piece of writing from your folder. Read through it and circle the first word of each new sentence. (*Give the students time to circle.*) What did you notice?

Tiara: I noticed most of my sentences began with different words.

Robert: Most of mine started with *I.*

Mrs. H-D: Today I'd like to show you a simple revision strategy that will help if you notice too many sentences are beginning the same way. Please turn in your notebooks to the revision section. At the top of the page please write "Rewriting Sentences." Today we will practice rewriting sentences. (*I write the following sentence on chart paper or whiteboard:* I munched on popcorn while I watched the movie.) I'd like you to rewrite this sentence. You may move, add, or delete words. (*I give the students a minute or two to rewrite the sentence.*) Would someone like to share their rewritten sentence?

Earl: *I munched on yummy popcorn while I watched a scary movie.*

Mrs. H-D: Earl, how did that vary your sentence beginning?

Earl: It didn't vary the beginning, but it made it more interesting. I told what kind of popcorn and movie.

Mrs. H-D: So you revised your sentence by adding words.

Earl: Right.

Mrs. H-D: Who else would like to share?

Paige: This is what I did. I switched the beginning and ending of the sentence.

Mrs. H-D: Tell me more.

Paige: Well, your sentence says *I munched on popcorn while I watched the movie.* My sentence starts out with *I watched the movie* and ends with *munched on popcorn.* I also left out a word. But I'm still noticing my sentence begins with *I.*

Mrs. H-D: I see what you did. You not only switched the beginning and ending, but you also deleted a word. Let's have one more person share.

Adele: I know how to vary the beginning and not start with *I.*

Mrs. H-D: Say more.

Adele: Well, I started my sentence with *while.* Instead of saying *I munched on popcorn while I watched the movie,* I rewrote it. Now it says, *While I watched the movie, I munched on popcorn.*

Mrs. H-D: All three of you rewrote the sentence in a different way. Rewriting sentences is a revision strategy. Varying sentence beginnings, adding and deleting words, and moving pieces around can make your sentences more interesting or just sound better. Today writers, I'd like you to find a sentence or two in the piece you are working on to rewrite. Good luck!

As a quick follow-up activity, put a sentence on the chalkboard and ask students to rewrite it. Here are some samples I've used with success:

- I love to run in the morning.
- Turtles swim in ponds, rivers, and lakes.
- My favorite color is periwinkle.
- Last summer we visited Washington, D.C.
- Learning about fractions is fun.

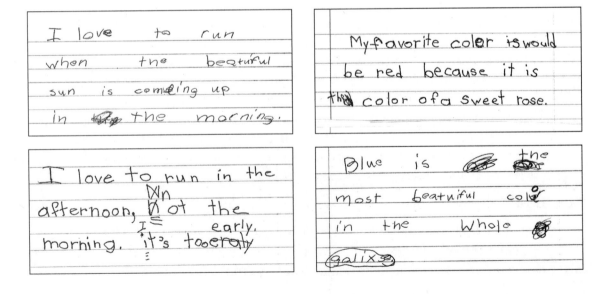

Problem ✳ *Student writing is not specific.*

Strategy ✳ **Add details and examples.**

Mrs. H-D: Sometimes when we reread our writing, we notice that it sounds a little vague, a little general. A reader might have questions and not understand what we're trying to say. When this happens, we can look for places where we can give more specific details, or maybe we can think of an example to show what we mean. When I was rereading my piece on bats earlier today, I realized I hadn't given many specific details. Let me reread it to you, and you can help me decide what details I should add.

I place my piece on the overhead, reread, and take suggestions on how to add details so the reader can picture bats. Once we've worked through the process together, I ask students to reread a piece they're working on, looking for places where more detail would be helpful.

Bats (my first draft)

When I was young, occasionally a bat flew around inside our house at night. I used to scream late at night when I heard the flapping of wings. I was afraid they would get in my hair, or even bite me like a vampire. But when I got older, I realized bats are fascinating creatures.

Did you know that bats are not blind? Bats look funny. They use sound to find their way. Bats are good because they eat lots of insects. Bats live in trees. Bats come out at night. Bats have babies.

If you would like to learn more about bats check out your local library for books such as Bats *by Lawrence Pringle.*

Fascinating Facts About Bats (my revised draft)

When I was young, occasionally a bat flew around inside our house at night. My dad suspected the bats entered the house when one of us was opening and closing the doors. My mom said bats at night were the result of the massive evergreen tree reaching for our roof. I used to scream and scream and scream when I'd hear the flapping of wings at night, fearing the bat would become entangled in my hair, or even suck my blood like a vampire. But as I grew older, I realized bats are fascinating creatures.

Did you know that bats are not blind? That's right. Bats can see and they can also hear. Bats use sound to find their way around. This is called echolocation. Echolocation helps bats hear everything, like tiny insects, rustling leaves, and falling twigs. It also helps them find their dinner. For dinner bats enjoy insects like mosquitoes, which helps us out. Some bats like fruit and frogs. And it is true some bats like blood.

Bats are unusual looking. I think they look like a mouse with wings. They have eyes like black pearls and fur. Hooked toes help bats hang upside down. Bats use their wings like humans use their arms and hands.

A cave, a tree, or even your house can be a home for a bat. Bats are nocturnal. That means bats are awake at night and sleep during the day.

That sounds like my mom. She did the same thing.

Baby bats drink their mother's milk. Baby bats can't fly for a few weeks after they are born. Once in awhile a baby bat ventures out with its mom. The mom carries the baby.

Yes! Bats are interesting creatures. If you would like to learn more about bats check out Bats! Strange and Wonderful *by Lawrence Pringle at your local library.*

As a follow-up activity, write vague sentences on the chalkboard and ask students to rewrite them, adding details or examples to make them more specific.

Teacher Sentence: I love to go to my grandma's.

Student Sentence: I love to go to my grandma's to swim, splash, and have fun.

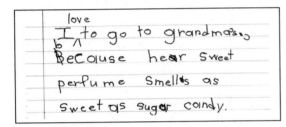

| love |
| I to go to grandmas, |
| Because hear sweet |
| perfume Smells as |
| sweet as sugar candy. |

| I love to go |
| to grant mas |
| because she gives |
| me (choclat), cookies |
| and creamy, sweet milk. |

Problem ✳ *Overuse of adjectives and adverbs.*

Strategy ✳ **Delete words.**

Mrs. H-D: Sometimes writers get carried away and use too many words to describe a person, object, or event. If readers understand what something is, there's no reason to spend extra words describing it. For instance, today I was writing about my recent trip to Washington. One of my favorite things about D.C. is the Smithsonian. It's so wonderful! I can think of many adjectives to describe it, and here's what I wrote: *When I visit Washington D.C., every year, I always tour the beautiful, wonderful Smithsonian.* When I reread this sentence, I realize that I don't need to say *beautiful* and *wonderful* before *Smithsonian.* That doesn't really add anything new or important to what I'm trying to say. I'm going to take those words out. In my next sentence I talk in particular about the Air and Space Museum, and I'll go into detail about the exhibits I saw there.

Today, I'd like you to choose a piece from your folder and reread carefully looking for places where you include extra adjectives and adverbs that don't really need to be there.

| When I visit Washing |
| ton D.C I always tour |
| the beautiful |
| Smithonian. |

| I visit Washington DC. |
| every year, I never miss |
| out on the tour of |
| the wonderful smithonian. |

As a follow-up activity, put a sentence with extraneous adjectives or adverbs on the board and ask students to revise to make it cleaner.

Teacher Sentence: The big, round, full moon shines on the very nice ocean water.

Student Sentence: The full moon shines on the ocean.

Problem ✳ Student writing lacks specific nouns and strong verbs.
Strategy ✳ Use strong vocabulary (verbs and nouns).

Mrs. H-D: Writers strive to use the very best words so readers can understand exactly what the writer wants to say. Sometimes when we're drafting, though, we use the first words that come to mind, and they might not necessarily be the best. As we reread and revise, it's a good idea to pay attention to the nouns and verbs we use in our drafts. Check each one to make sure it's specific and strong, so you create a clear picture and communicate your ideas. Listen to this sentence: *For Christmas Santa gave me lots of stuff.* Can anyone tell me what I got for Christmas?

Brandon: You got stuff. Since you didn't use specific words, none of us know what you got for Christmas.

Mrs. H-D: Say more about this, Brandon.

Brandon: If you told us what you actually got, like maybe a necklace or a book or a sweater, we would know what you're talking about. The word *stuff* doesn't help us to picture anything.

Mrs. H-D: So, Brandon, you are telling me I need to write specific nouns. How does this sound? *For Christmas, Santa gave me a box of chocolates, a red silk scarf, and a baby kitten named Sophie.*

Brandon: That sounds much better.

Mrs. H-D: Thank you. Today as you work on your writing, be on the lookout for nouns that don't show us anything specific. Try changing them to name something in particular, as I did by stating what kinds of gifts I got from Santa.

To help students understand revision, we must model by putting some of our own writing in front of students. Students are quite good at honestly critiquing someone else's writing, especially if it is their teacher's. Students need to talk about and explain their own thinking, and we must give them that time. Giving Brandon the opportunity to discuss my writing encouraged Tiara to revise my generic sentence as follows:

Tiara's sentence: *For Christmas, Santa got me a fur Real Friend cat and it was black and white like Chowder.*

Problem ✳ Students need to slow the moment down.
Strategy ✳ Add rich details.

In this lesson, I ask a student to help me by sharing one of his or her pieces with the class. Students usually love to do this, and they don't mind having their work used as a model. Of course, I always ask permission and let them know what will happen first, and if there's any hesitation, I find another student.

Mrs. H-D: Writers, I'm going to tell you a story about a possum. Are you ready?

Students: Yes!

Mrs. H-D: Last night I caught a possum. It was big, white, and very hungry. The End. Did you like my story?

Jess: Not really.

Alicia: What happened? How did you catch it?

Mrs. H-D: I see you have some questions. What exactly do you want to know?

Mallery: How did you catch the possum?

Ryan: Where was the possum?

Jess: How big was it?

Mrs. H-D: These are good questions, but I think I need a recorder. (*At this point I hand some sticky notes to a student and ask him or her to record the questions.*)

After a few more questions, I try my story again.

Mrs. H-D: Last night at about six o'clock, the phone rang. My neighbor told me she saw a possum crawl out from under my deck. She told me to look out the window. Sure enough, a big white possum headed straight for the neighbor's compost garden. For an hour, I watched that critter fill his belly. Slowly he headed back for his home under my deck. Now I knew Lucy, my little white dog, wouldn't get along well with a big white possum. I needed a plan. I ran in the house, put Lucy on her leash, and grabbed a broom and Lucy's cage. As soon as the possum saw Lucy, he played dead. Very carefully, I set Lucy's open cage in front of the possum. With the broom, I gave the possum a little scoot. He went right into Lucy's cage. Then I put the big white possum in my car and drove him down the road to a rather large wooded area. Then I let him go.
Now, how do you like my story?

Jess: Much better! It has more details.

Mallery: I think the questions we asked gave you more ideas.

Mrs. H-D: You are right. Yesterday, I asked Tiara to help me teach the lesson. She was having a little difficulty adding more information to her story. (*At this point, I call Tiara up and display her story on chart paper, where I had copied it in preparation for the lesson.*) Tiara, would you read your piece for us?

Tiara: (*Reading*) I'm afraid of spiders. I hate spiders.

Mrs. H-D: Writers, do you have any questions for Tiara?

Alicia: Why do you hate spiders?

Tiara: I think they are creepy.

Ryan: Do you scream when you see spiders?

Tiara: No. I call my brother.

Mallery: Why do you call your brother?

Tiara: Because he flushes them down the toilet.

    While the students ask questions, I record each question on a sticky note.

Mrs. H-D: Tiara, I'd like you to take the questions the other writers asked and see if you can add some more details to your story like I did with my story about the possum. Then tomorrow I would like you to share your revisions with the class.

I'm Afraid
by Tiara

I'm afraid of spiders. They are creepy. I hate spiders. When I see a spider I call my brother. He takes cares of them for me. He flushes them down the toilet. He says, "Good-bye spider!"

Problem ✳ *Students are writing telling sentences. Their writing lacks imagery and sensory detail.*

Strategy ✳ **Show, don't tell (or paint a picture).**

Mrs. H-D: Sometimes we know what we want to say in our writing, and we tell the reader our idea. But often just telling something is not very interesting or memorable. To make readers care about our writing and keep their interest, writers try to show their ideas, not just tell them. This is especially true when we want the reader to know how a character is feeling. Which sentence do you prefer:

Joseph was sad.

Tears streamed down Joseph's face when Ted grabbed the stuffed bear.

Allen: I like the second one. I know why Joseph is sad.

Luna: I like that one too. I can make a picture in my head. My brother has done that to me!

Mrs. H-D: We call this technique *show, don't tell*. Or you can think of it as painting a picture with words. Today as you write, look for places where you tell the reader something, and think about how you might show it instead.

Problem ✳ *Leads are generic and boring.*

Strategy ✳ **Change the beginning.**

    Many students start their pieces with standard leads such as *one day, my friend,* or *once upon a time*. These beginnings often fail to engage readers. When I notice this problem with students, I teach a literature-based mini-lesson on leads. I introduce students to different kinds of beginnings to give them more ideas about how to start their pieces. In this lesson, I've chosen two leads to share, an action lead and a setting lead. I often do this mini-lesson several times a year, sharing a variety of different types of leads with students.

Mrs. H-D: I've noticed that many writers in this class are starting their pieces the same way. I want to show you that you have many choices about how to begin; you don't always have to use the same lead over and over again. Remember how important a lead is. It's the first thing your readers read. You want it to grab their attention right away. Let's take a look at the leads from two of my favorite books, *The Red Racer* by Audrey Wood and *Night in the Country* by Cynthia Rylant. Listen first to the lead of *The Red Racer*.

> *Nona was pedaling to school on her old bicycle when the chain came off and the brakes jammed. "Look out!" Nona cried.*

What do you think of that?

Ryan: It's very exciting. It makes me want to keep reading.

Mrs. H-D: Yes, it is exciting. We call this an action lead, and you can begin that way too, by describing an action. Let's listen to another lead, this one from Cynthia Rylant's *Night in the Country*.

> *There is no night so dark, so black as night in the country. In little houses people lie sleeping and dreaming about daytime things, while outside–in the fields, and by the rivers, and deep in the trees–there is only night and nighttime things.*

What did you think of this lead?

Jessica: It was pretty. Not exciting like the first one, but I still want to keep reading.

Mrs. H-D: Yes, it's a very different kind of lead, but if it makes you want to keep reading, it's effective. Cynthia Rylant began by describing the setting of her story, and you can do that too. Today we heard two different ways to begin a piece of writing, with an action and with a description of setting. There are many other ways to do it. As you read, pay attention to how writers begin. You can borrow their techniques for your own writing. Today as you're writing, I'd like you to try a new lead for your piece. You could try an action lead, a setting lead, or another kind of lead you know about. Just make sure it's interesting and gets the readers' attention right away.

Trying out new leads works. Recently I had a fourth grader who rewrote her beginning in several different ways. Then she selected the one that she felt was the strongest.

Problem ✳ *Student writing fails to leave the reader with closure.*
Strategy ✳ **Change the ending.**

Second, third, and fourth graders all tend to think writing ends with either *THE END*, or *They lived happily ever after*. I've found that reading endings from literature is an effective way to expand students' repertoire for endings. Personal narrative is the easiest to teach because a personal experience piece ends with a thought or feeling. Present several ex-amples to your class. The following books are narratives that end with a thought or feeling.

- *Lucky Pennies and Hot Chocolate* by Carol Diggory Shields
- *I Like Me!* by Nancy Carlson
- *My Friend John* by Charlotte Zolotow
- *I Remember Papa* by Helen Ketteman
- *When I Was Young in the Mountains* by Cynthia Rylant

Allow students the opportunity to find their own examples of text that end with a thought or feeling, and encourage them to revise a piece of their own writing using this technique.

Problem ✳ ***Writing is unorganized. Writer may have lost his or her focus.***

Strategy ✳ **Cut-and-Tape to move parts around.**

Most students write from their hearts. Faith wrote about her grandmother. Anna wrote about her cat. David wrote about dinosaurs. Sometimes students are so passionate about the topic, they forget to organize their thoughts. When this happens, cut and tape is an easy strategy to teach. Moving parts around and reorganizing is less tedious with this method than students rewriting chunks of text. When you come across a piece of student writing in which chunks need to be reorganized, model cut-and-tape for the students. Faith was having a problem with organization. She needed to move parts around. I took a part of her writing and wrote it on chart paper. Then Faith and I used it for a cut-and-tape mini-lesson. Below is a part of Faith's piece about her grandmother.

> I love my grandma. She is nice. I have to stay with her every night because my mom and dad work. Sometimes we bake cookies. She reads me stories. Yesterday she took me to the dentist. I didn't have any cavities. I love my grandma. My mom works at the hospital. Dad works at a factory. He works third shift. Grandma likes sugar cookies the best. She lets me put frosting on the cookies.

Faith reads her story to the class. She reads with a smile. I know she is proud.

Mrs. H-D: Faith, you must really love your grandma. (*She nods.*) Yesterday when we were conferencing, I noticed you were having a little trouble. Will you tell us what you need our help with?

Faith: I have some sentences in the wrong place.

Mrs. H-D: Tell me more. How do you know your sentences are in the wrong place?

Faith: Well, I started talking about staying with my grandma while mom and dad go to work. I think I lost my focus because I started writing about making cookies and going to the dentist. Then I went back to jobs. It doesn't make sense.

Mrs. H-D: Would you like to rewrite your story?

Faith: (*Wide-eyed*) No, not all of it.

Mrs. H-D: Let me show you something I do with my writing. First, tell us what you want to change.

Faith: I need to put the part about where my mom and dad work at the top.

Mrs. H-D: Highlight the part you want to move. (*Faith highlights the sentence.*) Now I'm going to cut that part out. (*I cut apart the paper.*) Where do you want this part to go?

Faith: Right here. (*I tape the sentence where she indicates.*)

Mrs. H-D: There we go. Faith, please reread your piece now.

Faith: (*Reading*) *I love my grandma. She is nice. I have to stay with her every night because my mom and dad work. My dad works at a factory. My mom works at the hospital. Sometimes we bake cookies. Grandma likes sugar cookies the best. She lets me put frosting on the cookies. She reads me stories. Yesterday she took me to the dentist. I love my grandma.*

Mrs. H-D: It was a good idea to move that sentence, Faith. Your writing flows better now. Writers, when you want to move things around, don't be afraid to try it out because you think you'll have to rewrite a lot of words. Just cut and tape.

Cut-and-tape is easy for third and fourth graders, but second graders tend to use spider legs. Instead of cutting and taping, they simply write added details on separate strips of paper and then tape them on the place in their stories where they need to be inserted. See the example below.

Problem ✳ ***Writing is unclear, confusing, and doesn't make sense.***

Strategy ✳ **Reread for meaning.**

The easiest way to teach students to revise for meaning is by providing them time to read their writing aloud. Let students share with the whole class, partner read, read with you while conferencing, or read into a tape recorder and replay. It teaches them that rereading is an important part of revision.

To give students practice with rereading, I often use quickwrites. In a quickwrite, students write nonstop for a short period of time—two to three minutes for second graders, working up to five to seven minutes for older students—in response to open-ended words or phrases, such as *last night, I wish,* or *I wonder.* I always set a timer. When the timer chimes, I tell the students to read their writing in a whisper voice three times. When writers write fast they sometimes leave out words, repeat, or their writing lacks clarity. I encourage students as they reread to keep asking themselves, what am I trying to say? The process shows them the value of rereading for meaning. Some of the best writing I've received from students started with a quickwrite that was reread and thoughtfully revised.

> ### Problem ✳ *Writing lacks rhythm/cadence.*
> ### Strategy ✳ **Reread for sound (sentence fluency, cadence, word choice)**

Students learn the music of words not only by reading, but also by being read to. Immerse your students in poetry, song, and well written literature. We need to teach students to love the sounds of language. Dare to introduce young writers to simile, metaphor, and alliteration. The best way to teach students this is by modeling when you read. For instance, if you want your students to write using longer sentences, read them Kimberly Poulton's *Hello Willow.* Cynthia Rylant's *Mr. Putter and Tabby Pour the Tea* is a wonderful mentor book when teaching students the magic of three. *Canoe Days* by Gary Paulsen is rich in word choice, metaphor, and imagery. Read the text once for music and enjoyment, and again for calling attention to the writer's craft.

Frequently on the second read of a text, I will ask students to bring their writer's notebooks with them to our meeting area. I ask the students to list in their notebooks any words or phrases they love the sound of. Often a found poem surfaces. Word choices are so powerful, the only thing needed is simple revision.

Ask your students to find the parts in their writing that create music. Which words do you love the sound of? Which parts create cadence? If others read your writing, what found poems will they discover?

✳ Sharing Revision Strategies

After teaching any of the lessons I describe above, I ask students to give the strategy a try in their writing that day. To encourage them to continue to use the strategies, I prepare a large sheet of paper often used to cover bulletin boards and section it into large squares. Then I call students together for a mini-lesson that goes something like this:

Mrs. H-D: We've been working a lot on our writing, and we've discussed several revision strategies we can use to make our writing stronger. Today I want to review the strategies we've talked about. Let's record the strategies we've discussed on this chart. Can anyone suggest a strategy?

Jayden: Using specific nouns.

Mrs. H-D: Good one. I'll write that here. (*I write "Specific Nouns" in the first square on the chart.*) Another?

Jessica: Rewriting leads?

Mrs. H-D: Yes. I'll add that.

Allen: How about strong, active verbs?

Mrs. H-D: Excellent.

I continue until students finish adding strategies.

Mrs. H-D: I want us to use this chart to remind us of the strategies that are available to us. I also want us to talk about our writing, especially our revision, so when you use one of the strategies on our chart, please put a sticky note with your name on it under the strategy. Then at share time, you can talk about how you used the strategy in your writing. And we'll continue to add revision strategies to the chart as we learn more.

Revision Strategies

Adding a word or words	Deleting a word or words	Rewriting a sentence	Show not Tell	Adding details	Using strong vocabulary

Students love the idea of the chart and eagerly sign up when they use a strategy. For instance, when Brandon changed his beginning on his whale story, he immediately signed up to share. Many students willingly attempt revision if they know they will have a chance to share how they made their writing stronger. I firmly believe that if we provide students with many types of sharing opportunities, it encourages them to focus on the process of revision.

Chapter 2 Review

- Use a notebook to teach revision strategies.
- Practice the strategies.
- Model revision through mini-lessons.
- Provide students with opportunities to share their revisions.

Chapter 3

Practicing Revision on Other People's Writing

Chapter 2 provided you with daily revision strategies and lessons. The purpose of individually teaching these strategies is to help students develop an understanding of what revision looks like. When Adele reads her piece of writing to Audrey and she hears herself say, "I left some words out; this doesn't make sense," hopefully she'll have one of those golden moments where she'll understand…*yes, I'm revising!*

During writing workshop, most direct instruction is accomplished through mini-lessons that are designed to address the day-to-day needs of student writers. Conferencing, anecdotal notes, and reviewing student writing folders guide these mini-lessons, and students practice what they've learned that day in their own writing. Occasionally, however, I find it useful for students to set aside their own writing for short periods of time while they explore revision practices by working with other people's writing. Their exploration helps them gain a deeper understanding of revision and writers' craft.

After students have practiced some of the individual revision strategies on their own writing, I take a few days to delve into a focus lesson. A focus lesson engages the whole class in the study of a published piece of writing, often a picture book. Every student receives a copy of the text, which is read aloud, reread, and critically discussed over several days. Students analyze and respond to the text by marking it up and identifying the qualities of excellent writing. Then the teacher and students compose a criteria chart of the literary techniques the author used to craft the writing into a quality piece.

Focus lessons require more time, yet they provide the opportunity for in-depth conversation about craft. Focus lessons encourage meaningful discussion about an author's work; students can then use the insights gained through such study in their own writing.

Revision Centers

Georgia Heard's book *The Revision Toolbox* has a chapter titled "Revision Centers." She created centers in a fourth-grade classroom using some of these same strategies, giving students the opportunity to explore revision more deeply on their own. The centers are a perfect idea because students love independent learning.

The following focus lessons will allow students an opportunity to practice revision, but don't be limited to these. Use them as a model for your own focus lessons on topics of interest to you and your students.

Focus Lesson 1: Revising Someone Else's Work

Scarecrow by Cynthia Rylant is a beautiful book rich in vocabulary, imagery, and sentence structure. First, I read the book so students can enjoy the story, especially the language. On the second read, I ask students to listen closely for words or phrases they love the sound of. I tell them to put their hand across their heart when they hear the words they love the sound of, and to hold them there until the story ends. After the story ends, I ask them to share the words held close to their hearts. I ask third- and fourth-grade students to jot their words or phrases in their notebooks.

Mrs. H-D: Who would like to share first? (*As students share, I record their responses on chart paper.*)

Karly: pie-pan hands

Timmy: his gentleness

Nathan: chat

Jenna: mammoth pumpkins

Josh: like lace

Landon: brushing his borrowed

Cori: long slow thoughts

Mrs. H-D: My favorite is *rained and snowed and blossomed and wilted and yellowed and greened and vined.* Cynthia Rylant knows how to craft just the right words. Now, I want you to think about some things. If you made a scarecrow, what would it wear? Where would it live? What would it see? Take a few moments to imagine what your scarecrow would be like.

Many students will want to respond immediately, but I allow two full minutes of think time before I accept any answers. I encourage students to close their eyes and visualize a scene. After students share their responses orally, I give them about five minutes to sketch their scarecrow and its surroundings. Then I move into the next part of the lesson.

Mrs. H-D: I'd like to share a piece of writing with you that a student shared with me.

I give each student a copy of the following story and ask everyone to read it silently.

The Scarecrow

There is a scarecrow in my grandfather's field. He is a cool scarecrow. Birds don't like him. Scarecrows see lots of things. Someday I'm going to have a scarecrow.

Mrs. H-D: Writers, what do you think?

Jenna: It's short and choppy.

Mrs. H-D: Say more.

Jenna: It doesn't flow. There are too many short sentences and not any long sentences.

Josh: The sentences are telling. They don't show.

Timmy: Right. The words don't create a picture in your mind.

Mrs. H-D: I agree. Josh or Timmy, how would you make one of these sentences show?

Josh: Where the author wrote *scarecrows see lots of things*, I'd put something like a *scarecrow sees the full moon*.

Timmy: Or *a scarecrow sees the raccoons attack the garbage when there is a full moon.*

Mrs. H-D: These sentences are much more specific and descriptive, as we noticed Cynthia Rylant's were. Now, writers, this is what I would like you to do. I want you to revise this student's work. You may use any of the revision strategies we have discussed during writing workshop. You may add, delete, move, or rewrite. Please feel free to cut and tape. Some of you may want to add spider legs (*see page 22*). Please make sure your revision piece has a clear beginning, middle, and end. Have fun!

During sharing time, ask the students to share their revised stories. You may want them to share only one or two examples of revision strategies. Encourage students to explain how Cynthia Rylant's story *Scarecrow* influenced their revision.

Focus Lesson 2: Revising in the Style of a Published Author

The next lesson gives students an opportunity to revise a piece of writing in the style of a published author. Choose a piece by an author you and your students love; then write a bland piece on the same topic.

Let's Go Home by Cynthia Rylant is the book I use for this focus lesson. This book is about a home and what makes a home special. There are many kinds of houses, but this piece focuses on the living that is done in each room of a home. Since most living areas have a kitchen, I decide upon this room. At first, my thoughts were steered toward a bedroom, but many children live in small living areas where they don't have a bedroom. Some of my students sleep on a couch, sleeping bag, or a mattress in a living room, so I decided the kitchen would be more appropriate. The following is my bland piece about a kitchen. It generally follows the format of Rylant's description of a kitchen.

Everyone likes the kitchen. Kitchens have canisters, and bread, and sugar. Kitchens are wonderful. A kitchen has a refrigerator. Some are old and new. Some have a freezer. There is usually a sink. Some sinks have a window. Kitchens smell good when cookies are baked. People meet in the kitchen. Moms make lunches in the kitchen. People talk in the kitchen. People miss their kitchens when they are far away. People like to drink warm tea in their kitchen.

Mrs. H-D: Writers, please read my piece about a kitchen.

I give students time to read the piece.

Mrs. H-D: In one of Cynthia Rylant's texts, she writes about the rooms in a house. One of the rooms she writes about is a kitchen. Her writing inspired me to write about my own kitchen. Many of the items mentioned (*refrigerator, sink, window, cookies, tea*) are included in the text I handed you. But my text isn't as good as hers. Knowing Cynthia Rylant from our author studies, what is missing?

Brenna: Strong verbs.

Mrs. H-D: Give me some examples.

Anna: Well, like the word she used about the snake in *When I Was Young in the Mountains—draped.*

Mrs. H-D: Yes, she does use strong verbs.

Nik: Feelings. The words don't show feelings. She always writes in a way that you know she cares about her topic.

Mrs. H-D: Please be more specific.

Nik: Like when she writes about growing up in the mountains. She says something like *that was always enough.* I mean she never wanted to be anywhere else. She must have really cared about the mountains. I mean I sure would like to go to other places.

Mrs. H-D: I agree. This piece we are critiquing lacks emotion and a deep caring for the topic. Is there anything else?

Matt: Word choice. Like the piece doesn't have any great language. I know I need to give an example. Let me think. . . . Those words you love so much.

Mrs. H-D: I've got it! When she said the old people *smelled of sweet milk.* I do love those words. By the way, the old people have names, *Mr. and Mrs. Crawford.*

Tiara: I know something else. This piece doesn't really appeal to the senses. There needs to be something more about the cookies and tea. It needs to make the reader hear and taste and smell more.

Mrs. H-D: How might you do that if you were revising this piece?

Lexi: Instead of *cookies*, I might say *sugar cookies.*

Chris: I would say *warm green tea.* That's what my grandma drinks.

Scott: I would write more about why people miss their kitchens. My mom would miss her kitchen because it is where she spends most of her time. She likes to bake pies.

Mrs. H-D: Now writers, it is your turn to practice revising. I'd like you to take this piece, which lacks feeling, word choice, and overall appeal to the senses and revise it. Once again you may use any of the revising strategies we have discussed. After your revised pieces are complete and you have an opportunity to share, I will read you the portion of the text where Cynthia Rylant writes about a kitchen. Then we will do some comparing and contrasting. Have fun!

In this lesson, students were discussing the qualities of good writing. They were talking about emotion, senses, and language—the elements that enhance style and voice. They were able to identify what was missing and think about how they might revise, drawing on their knowledge of an accomplished writer and her work. For second, third and fourth graders to understand the kind of revision that needs to be done is an accomplishment in itself. After the students shared their revised pieces, I read them the text about a kitchen from *Let's Go Home*. As a community of writers we compared and contrasted our writing to Cynthia Rylant's. The students found their writing had threes, similes, and organization as Cynthia Rylant's does. Most students agreed their writing differed in the ability to play with words like Rylant. And many students felt her writing sounds musical due to flow, rhythm, and cadence. As a class we decided we needed to work on this in our writing.

In our kitchen, the floors are speckled. Blue, red, and black spots dot the floor. My brother and I like to make ourselves dizzy by turning round and round on the kitchen floor. Mom and Dad always tell us not to do this. They say we might get hurt. But we don't care! When the kitchen is quiet, and the sink light is lit, my brother and I sneak in the kitchen. We start turning like tops, tornadoes, and wheels. We spin and spin and spin. Then we lay on our backs and stare at the ceiling. The colors are like a kaleidoscope. Suddenly, our dad's voice booms. He wonders if we are making ourselves dizzy again. Our kitchen is the best room in the house.

—fourth-grade student

My dad says our kitchen looks like a big sunflower. The walls are yellow. We have sunflowers on the tablecloth, curtains, and napkins. Sometimes my mom wears perfume that smells like sunflowers. When she wears her black dress with the big yellow sunflowers, we know how much she loves sunflowers. She likes to bake cookies in our sunflower kitchen. One time when we came home from school, my mom had baked sugar cookies. The kitchen smelled so, so good. The cookies were big and soft and warm. She frosted them. The cookies looked like sunflowers. My mom loves her sunflower kitchen.

—third-grade student

Focus Lesson 3: Modeling Revision on Your Own Work

One of the most powerful approaches to teaching writing is modeling for your students. They need to see how you select topics, organize thoughts, draft pieces, revise, and edit. For many teachers this is a challenge. I find that keeping a writer's notebook is a great help in this regard. I buy cheap composition books and keep one in my car, a small one in my purse, one in the kitchen, one in my office, and one at my bedside. You see, when I get an idea, or start wondering, or hear words that I love, I need to write them down, or I'll forget. Ralph Fletcher's *A Writer's Notebook* is a must not only for students, but also for teachers. Once you read this book, you'll keep notebook after notebook. My notebooks provide me with writing that I can show to my students.

My students see me as a writer when I model selecting ideas from my writer's notebook. I demonstrate organization by developing plans. I draft in front of the students, usually on an overhead. I revise, inviting students to critique my work. I edit by copyediting, and then handing my work to one of my students to co-edit.

The first time I ever presented this lesson to students, I wasn't sure of the responses I would receive. Since I spend a lot of time at the lake, my writer's notebook was full of entries about animals—raccoons, red squirrels, snakes, and frogs. I chose to write about a frog. I quickly did a CSP, a prewriting activity I use with my students. *C* is for *character*; *S* is for *setting*; and *P* is for *problem*. The character was a naughty little frog. The setting was a pond with reeds and lilypads. The problem was that the little frog didn't listen. It took two days to draft the story on the overhead. The first day I drafted for approximately ten minutes in front of the class. I wrote, deleted, and added. While I wrote, I talked to myself. The students needed to see me thinking, fighting writer's block, and revising.

My Think Aloud

I write: *Little Frog lived by a pond.*

I say: No Little Frog lived by a beautiful pond. Let's see, now I need to describe the pond. I need to show my readers the beauty of the pond. I think I'll describe the setting in threes.

I write: *The weeds were tall. The water, crystal clear. Wildflowers covered the bank.*

I say: I think I'll cross out *covered*. I need a stronger verb. I think I'll try *sprinkled*. Yes, this sounds better. *Wildflowers sprinkled the bank.*

I write: *Little Frog couldn't swim very well. He loved to jump.*

I say: I want to use some dialogue, but not a lot. What could Mother say? I think I'll try this…

I write: *"Little Frog, all that jumping is going to lead to big trouble!" Mother Frog yelled.*

I say: I need a stronger word than *yelled*. Mother Frog is quite serious. I think I'll take out the word *yelled* and put in *warned*.

The second day I drafted quietly during their writing time. The third day I asked students to critique my piece of writing. I wasn't sure this would work. My concern was that the students might hesitate giving the critical feedback my writing needed. After all, I was their writing teacher. I was pleasantly surprised for several reasons. One was their honesty. The other was the quality of their suggestions. Below is a copy of my first draft and the feedback the students gave me.

Little Frog Learns a Lesson

Little Frog lived by a beautiful pond. The weeds were tall. The water crystal clear. Wildflowers sprinkled the bank. Little Frog couldn't swim very well. He loved to jump. "Little Frog, all that jumping is going to lead to big trouble!" Mama Frog warned.

Little Frog did not listen. One summer afternoon he found a lovely lilypad. He jumped little jumps. He jumped big jumps. When Little Frog was jumping enormous jumps, a strong gust of wind carried Little Frog through the air and into the water.

"Help!" croaked Little Frog. He began to sink. Suddenly Grandpa Turtle swam by. "Climb on Little Frog!" Grandpa Turtle gently put Little Frog on the lilypad.

No more jumping for Little Frog. Now he practices swimming every day.

Before asking for critical feedback, ask students to give appreciations for the things the writer has done well. A positive approach builds safety in the writing community.

Mrs. H-D: Writers, please give three appreciations for the things I did well in this piece.

Lexi: I appreciate the beginning. The way you used a setting to capture our attention.

Mrs. H-D: Thank you. Who has another appreciation?

Matt: I appreciate the way you have a beginning and end. (*Notice this student doesn't say anything about the middle.*)

Mrs. H-D: Thanks. One more.

Brenna: I appreciate some of the verbs like *sprinkled* and *croaked*.

Mrs. H-D: Thanks. Now who has a question or suggestion?

> As students make suggestions or ask questions, either write them on your rough draft or on sticky notes. This not only models for students the value of their feedback, but it also helps you as a writer to address these issues.

Justin: Mrs. H-D, you need more details in the middle. When the frog is jumping, the sentences just tell. They don't give much information.

Mrs. H-D: That is a good suggestion. I was struggling with the middle. Could you be a little more specific?

Justin: Maybe the frog could jump on three different lilypads. You need to give the reader more information about each event.

Mrs. H-D: Who else has a question?

Mark: Something doesn't make sense. Why did you write Grandpa Turtle rather than Grandpa Frog?

Mrs. H-D: (*I laugh*) Good question. I don't know why. I imagine I wrote Grandpa Turtle because I was writing fast.

Megan: I think your beginning should paint more of a picture for the reader. For example, you might talk about the colors of the wildflowers. Are the flowers purple, yellow, or blue? Were there any other animals around the pond?

Mrs. H-D: From your comments, I think I need to do some serious revision. Writers, after I work on this, would you be willing to let me share again?

Students: Sure!

The fourth day I work quietly on the revisions as students are writing. I focus my work on the students' suggestions and questions. It is paramount that students know their feedback is vital to the writing community, and that teachers as well as classmates value essential feedback. On the fifth day I present the revisions to students once again. As you can see, this lesson will take approximately a week. It is an important lesson because students not only experience seeing you work as a writer through the entire writing process, but they also see revision as a vital part of the process. This lesson has always been successful and enjoyable for both the students and me.

Here is the revised Frog story.

Little Frog lived in a pond with squawking geese, quiet turtles, and an occasional dragonfly. Wildflowers, the colors of an afternoon rainbow, decorated the edges of the pond. A blue heron nibbled among the tall weeds. Lilypads cluttered the murky water.

Little Frog didn't know how to swim, but he loved to jump. Every day when Mother Frog taught him to swim, Little Frog didn't listen. He jumped—little jumps, big jumps, and enormous jumps. Mother Frog warned Little Frog that all that jumping was going to lead to big trouble.

One summer afternoon while Little Frog was napping on a nearby lilypad, a dragonfly darted by. Little Frog was annoyed. So guess what he did? He started to jump on that lilypad. At first he was careful. He jumped quiet jumps. Then that dragonfly darted right back in front of Little Frog. Little Frog was more annoyed. So he jumped bigger jumps. Little Frog bounced all over that lilypad. His legs were slippery and wet. Once again the dragonfly darted by Little Frog. But this time Little Frog heard dragonfly giggle. Boy, was Little Frog mad. He had a plan. He would jump many enormous jumps until he smacked dragonfly's silvery wings.

When Little Frog saw dragonfly approaching, he jumped little jumps. He jumped big jumps, and when he jumped an enormous jump, Little Frog jumped so high and so far, he landed splat in the middle of the murky water.

Gurgle, gurgle, gurgle! Help, help, help! Little Frog croaked. Now it just so happened Uncle Turtle was sunning himself on the pond's edge. He opened one eye when he heard Little Frog wailing. Slowly Uncle Turtle paddled to the middle of the pond. He could hear Little Frog coughing and sputtering. "Climb on, Little Frog," Uncle Turtle said in a very serious voice. Little Frog clutched Uncle Turtle's shell as they swam through the murky water. For a long time Uncle Turtle and Little Frog didn't say a word. Gently Uncle Turtle dropped Little Frog on his lilypad.

No more jumping for Little Frog. Now he practices swimming every day.

When I presented the revised Little Frog story, students felt I had improved in the following three areas: the beginning painted more of a picture, the elaboration in the middle of the story was more interesting, and one student felt Uncle Turtle was more appropriate than Grandpa Turtle. Most students felt the end was abrupt. It needed work. I agreed.

The focus lessons in this chapter allow students to experiment with revision on another writer's work, which is often easier for inexperienced writers than revising their own writing. The experience can give students the confidence and motivation to revisit and revise their own work.

Chapter 3 Review

- Teach revision through Focus Lessons.
- Share excellent literature with students.
- Encourage students to listen for words and phrases they love the sound of.
- Model your own writing and ask students for appreciations, questions, and suggestions.
- Explore revision by having students revise other writers' work.

Chapter 4

Expanding Revision Repertoires With Mentor Texts

Whenever I consult in schools, the one thing teachers ask for are titles of books. As a teacher, I believe quality literature is essential to my job. Take away the fancy easel, the carpet, the telephone, or my desk, but don't ever take my books. If my classroom was stripped of everything, I know I could provide outstanding opportunities for students as long as I had my books.

For as long as I can remember, I have collected children's books. My classroom is full of books. My home office is full of books. I purchase books as gifts. Friends and family members buy me books and bookstore gift cards. Students and their parents purchase books for our classroom library. In our classroom library you'll find narrative, nonfiction, poetry, and every possible genre students enjoy. To put it simply, in order to teach reading and writing you have to know books. Here are a few suggestions to help you learn titles:

- Visit the public library. Ask the librarian to notify you when new titles arrive.
- Ask your school librarian to display new titles for the faculty. Some schools have afternoon teas at which teachers leisurely review new literature.
- Visit the children's section of your local bookstore. Gather new titles, and read, read, read!
- Encourage your principal to provide the faculty with the opportunity to share titles at teacher meetings.
- Share books at grade-level meetings or during collaboration.
- Review titles on student book order forms.
- Subscribe to *Horn Book*, or other literary periodicals.
- Know your favorite authors and their works.

What does this have to do with revision? Everything! You can't help your students revise their beginning, change their ending, or use rich language unless you have the tools. And the tools are the books you have at your fingertips. Literature provides options, possibilities, and models for writing. For example, when a student begins a personal narrative piece with *Hi! My name is* _____, I immediately grab three texts—one that begins with a question, one that begins with dialogue, and one that begins with action. We read and discuss how the authors begin each of their pieces. Then I encourage the writer to select one type of beginning that might work for her piece and give it a try. If I didn't have the books and know the writer's craft, I wouldn't be able to help my students with meaningful revision.

How do I get all these books? I always pay full price. Here are a few other ways:

- Visit garage sales.
- Order from student book orders.
- Put titles on birthday or holiday lists.
- Encourage parents and friends to donate used books.

I started my collection in the same fashion. My husband used to cringe when I told him I was on my way to the bookstore. He eventually got the message. One of my Christmas gifts last year was a $200 gift certificate to our local bookstore. My students enjoyed this gift as much as I did.

Mentor Books

In her book *What You Know by Heart*, Katie Wood Ray refers to Cynthia Rylant's books *The Scarecrow* and *The Whales* as touchstone texts. She defines touchstone texts as books full of curriculum potential. She says a book becomes a touchstone text when you have read it over and over and know the writing so well that you see the potential to develop your own curriculum lessons. She knows these books so well that she is able to teach more than 50 curriculum lessons from both books.

I call Rylant's books my mentor books. I've named these books mentor texts because I like to think of published authors as the mentors for my classroom writing workshop. Let me give you an example. If some of my students wish to write chapter books, I pull Cynthia Rylant's *Mr. Putter and Tabby Pour the Tea*. The first read is for enjoyment. The second and third reads, we look at Rylant's craft. Together we study things like organization, strong verbs, and the way she creates cadence.

Every teacher needs to have mentor books. I also think it is important for us to find a mentor text for each of the genres we teach. For example, if a student is writing a fictional narrative, I need a mentor book that I can refer to. We can't help students with revision unless we understand the literary qualities of the genres students are writing in.

> **Mentor Text**
> *Lucky Penny and Hot Chocolate*
> by Carol Diggory Shields
>
> Writing Craft Lessons:
> - Beginning, middle, end
> - Organization
> - Voice
> - Sentence fluency—short and long sentences, use of three
> - Varied sentence beginnings
> - Strong vocabulary
> - Sensory details
> - Alliteration
> - An ending with a twist
> - Elaboration
> - Humor
> - Comparison

How do you choose a mentor text? It's an individual choice. I recommend reading widely and paying attention to the books that grab you. Actively search out one author you would like to have as a mentor. Choose a picture book, a piece of poetry, or a newspaper article. Do some deep reading that allows you to meaningfully look at the author's work. One of the things I do when I find a style of writing I like is to type the text out. This allows me to look deeply at the writer's craft by marking, circling, or highlighting strong vocabulary, organization, and vivid details. After I've read and marked the text, I make a list of all the things I could teach my students from the text. I've taught myself so much about writing from studying text. Fine authors know their craft. They love language and they write from their hearts. Somewhere inside, life provided them with an intrinsic gift. Many of us don't have the natural ability to write well. Studying text allows us to learn the writing craft. For me, it has been the single most important method of learning craft. As a result of identifying the traits of quality writing, I am able to do a better job of teaching revision.

Mentor Texts at Work

After you find a mentor text, order a copy for each student in your class. I save book club points for this purpose. If you can't afford this, either type the text and give each student a copy, or make an overhead. When studying craft, it is important for students to have the material in front of them.

Here's an example of how a mentor text can support and enrich teaching. While working with a group of fourth graders, Tedra noticed her students' writing seemed choppy. Together we examined the writing samples. The first thing Tedra pointed out was that sentences tended to begin the same way. Sentences repeatedly began with words such as *I, my, then, she,* and *he.* Collaboratively, we decided to plan a mini-lesson on varying sentence beginnings. Since Tedra had read Gary Paulsen's *Canoe Day* for a read-aloud that morning, we decided to revisit this picture book for our mini-lesson. The next day we gave each student a copy of the text. As Tedra read it aloud, students highlighted the first few words of each sentence. When she finished reading, Tedra asked students to share what they noticed about the way Gary Paulsen varied his sentence beginnings.

Tedra: Tell us what you noticed about the sentence beginnings in this story.

Will: I noticed that the first two sentences begin with the word *sometimes.*

Tedra: Why do you think he did that?

Will: I'm not sure.

Bradon: He didn't start two sentences with *sometimes* because there is a dash after *wing.* I think he had more to say, and he used *sometimes* twice because he wanted the readers to know how still it really is. I think it is like right before a thunderstorm when it gets quiet and the wind isn't blowing.

Lexi: Gary Paulsen does begin two sentences in a row with the word *come.*

Tedra:	Why do you think he did that, Lexi?
Lexi:	I think the author wanted the readers to know that the mother deer was worried. She wants the fawn to leave now because it could be in danger.
Tedra:	What else did you notice?
Sam:	I noticed that most of the sentences begin with different words like *sunfish, ahead, across, then*.
Tedra:	Why do you think the author used the words *ahead, across,* and *then*?
Sam:	So his writing flows?
Tedra:	That's right. Those are transition words—they keep the writing moving.
Jenna:	I noticed he used three and all of the sentences started with *a*.
Tedra:	Say more.
Jenna:	Well, he writes *a fox drinks, a raccoon turns,* and *a snake moves*. But after he writes the sentence about the fox, he puts in a short sentence about the fox that begins with *then*.
Tedra:	Why did the author put a short sentence?
Jenna:	Because when you use short and long sentences it helps the flow of the writing.
Sam:	It makes a rhythm.
Tedra:	Today I heard you discussing many reasons why writers vary their sentence beginnings. I heard you say writers vary sentence beginnings for flow, transition, and even for emphasis. Jenna mentioned authors sometimes begin sentences with the same word to help them create a pattern of three. Now I'd like you to return to the piece you are working on and highlight your sentence beginnings. If your sentence beginnings are not varied and your writing seems choppy, ask yourself how you might use transition words to help your writing flow. You might even try starting three sentences with the same word to create a rhythm. Good luck!

In this instance, Tedra was able to call upon Paulsen's book to help her address a particular need of students. That's the beauty of mentor books—we can turn to them again and again to teach students about various craft elements.

To help you get started, I have listed possible mentor texts for the various genres I teach. Read them for enjoyment first. Then study the text. Notice the idea, organization, language, and elaboration. Ask yourself: Am I passionate about the book? Do I want to delve into it, exploring the crafting techniques the author uses? Remember, knowing books and authors is a journey. The books a teacher uses in the classroom should excite both the students and the teacher. It would be easy for me to generate a list of 50 books for each genre. But if you run out and purchase those same books, it does not guarantee that you'll have the same passion for those titles as I do. I offer you a challenge. I will share one of my mentor books for each of the following genres. The challenge is for you to find two more mentor books for each genre.

Personal Narrative * *I Like Me!* by Nancy Carlson

Fictional Narrative * *The Red Racer* by Audrey Wood

Poetry * *Winter Eyes* by Douglas Florian

Chapter Books * *Mr. Putter and Tabby Pour the Tea* by Cynthia Rylant

Fairy Tale * *Snow White in New York* by Fiona French

Cumulative Stories * *The Napping House* by Audrey Wood

Memoir * *I Remember Papa* by Helen Ketteman

Biography * *The Story of Ruby Bridges* by Robert Coles

Informational Narrative * *Snowflake Bentley* by Jacqueline Briggs Martin

Informational Expository * *Arctic Foxes and Red Foxes* by Graham Meadows

Expository Narrative * *The Popcorn Book* by Tomie dePaola

How-To Writing * *Making Shadow Puppets* by Jill Bryant and Catherine Heard

Persuasive Writing * *Should We Have Pets? A Persuasive Text*
by Sylvia Lollis and Joyce W. Hogan

Explanation Writing * *From Wax to Crayon* by Robin Nelson

Chapter 4 Review

- Read and review books for children.
- Collect books.
- Choose mentor books.
- Develop a repertoire of lessons for mentor books.

Chapter 5

The Next Step
Editing and Proofreading

An interesting discovery I've made is that students not only revise naturally, but they edit naturally as well. I didn't realize this until I required students to write their rough drafts with black pens. When students could no longer erase, they crossed out, drew arrows, or wrote above and below their writing. At night, as I reviewed their pieces, I was amazed. They were editing! The process had been invisible to me before, but it was happening.

My students' writing demonstrated their knowledge that even though writing is a cycle, it is not linear. Students provided with regular writing opportunities move in and out of the cycle, especially if they are encouraged to reread their work. As they write and rewrite, they attend to the mechanics of writing, which is editing. They capitalize, punctuate, and fix grammatical errors every time they reread.

I was pleased to notice my students editing on their own, but I also wanted to ensure that they edited purposefully before publication. I asked myself what it was that I wanted my students to accomplish when it came to editing during that stage of the writing process. After careful thought and reflection, I decided on two areas. The first was spelling. Students need to return to their writing and be accountable for correcting spelling errors. The second was that my students return to their writing and reread for their mechanical errors. This is when I decided to teach them how to copyedit. When students copyedit, they use red pens, which allows me to see that students have revisited their work for mechanics. In this chapter, I share the routines and procedures I use to help my students edit for spelling and mechanics.

Getting Started: Spelling

Spelling is always an issue. Students need to know that they don't have to spell every word correctly in order to write. I can't tell you how many times I've visited classrooms and observed students with a clean sheet of paper in front of them. It doesn't matter if they are students in second, third, or fourth grade. If I position myself eye-level with the student and ask if there is something he or she needs help with, the typical response is

"I don't know how to spell _____." Yet the writer is not even going to use the word until the end of the first paragraph. In order to avoid this problem, I teach this mini-lesson early in the year, before students ever start drafting. It goes something like this:

Mrs. H-D: Since I've been teaching writing, one of things I've noticed is that some writers struggle with drafting because they are worried that they won't be able to spell a word correctly. Writing time is important, and you don't want to waste one of those precious writing minutes worrying about how to spell a word. Because I want you to focus on your ideas and drafting, this is what I would like you to do. Whenever you come to a word that is tricky, try to stretch that word out. For example, if you want to write "terrifying," you would stretch it out and write down the sounds you hear. (*I sound out the word and write the sounds on the board.*) If you are not sure you spelled the word correctly, immediately circle it. I'm not sure this looks right, so I'm going to circle it. (*I circle my sound-spelling.*)

Just think about it. If you use the circling technique, you not only have an opportunity to select interesting vocabulary for your writing, but you also won't waste minutes you could be using to develop your ideas. Later on, we'll discuss some ways to figure out the correct spelling of a word, but for now, just try stretching out words and circling any that you're not sure of.

Once students catch on to this technique, you will find them using it whenever written language is required in math, reading, and other subject areas. The perk for teachers is they don't become bogged down with students continuously asking how to spell words. Students learn to focus on the content of the piece.

A Purpose for Editing: Publishing

Once students complete drafts of several different pieces, I ask them to find a quiet place in the room and to reread their drafts, searching for the one they feel is their best, one they would like to take to the public. By the public, I mean anywhere outside our classroom writing community. An instructional facilitator I work with teaches her students the importance of editing by telling them the farther the piece travels out into the world, the more perfected it needs to be. Once students understand the importance of publishing, it is time for them to select a piece and to move into the editing process.

Editing for Spelling

The first thing I like to have students deal with when editing is spelling. Personally, I do not require students to correct every misspelled word before a piece is presented for publishing. Frequently used grade-level words are non-negotiable; they must be correct. Beyond that, I'm flexible. I believe that determining how many words are corrected is the responsibility of the teacher and the writing community. Students need to be included in the decision. It may be a group choice or an individual choice. I've noticed some writers will correct every circled word, whereas a poor speller may feel overwhelmed by the same number of circled words. In this situation, I negotiate with the student to determine how many words should be corrected.

There are two important points to keep in mind. The first is the process. Ultimately we want students to understand the process of editing, rereading writing with a critical eye as we prepare it for an audience. The second is that the teacher is the final editor. When a piece is submitted for publishing, I look it over and decide if sufficient effort went into the editing process. If the writer attempted to correct as many spelling errors as possible, or fixed the agreed upon words, then it is submitted for publishing. Let me demonstrate the lesson I use to teach students to correct their spelling.

In teaching, my purpose is always to put myself out of a job. I don't want students depending on me. I want them to become independent learners. In order to build independence, I need to facilitate lessons that encourage responsibility. In terms of editing, this means providing students with the tools and strategies to edit effectively on their own. To introduce spelling strategies, I write a copy of the spelling checklist students will use on a chart so we all can see. Then I choose a writer who is ready to edit for spelling to help with the lesson.

Mrs. H-D: Yesterday when I was conferencing with some of you, I noticed some writers are ready to correct their spelling. I've asked Adele to help us with today's lesson. Before we begin, I'd like to do some brainstorming. You know how important it is for each of you to become an independent learner. This is what I would like to think about. Most of you have been circling words you weren't sure how to spell or interesting vocabulary you stretched out to use in your writing. As you get ready to publish your work, you need to correct these spelling words. What are some ways you can think of to find out how to spell these words correctly? Keep in mind, you can't ask me.

> One of the guidelines for students to follow during writing workshop time is not to erase. They should cross out. Erasing wastes time and does not allow the teacher to see how students naturally revise and edit.

Write all the responses on a large chart for later use.

Sam: Look in the dictionary.

Rachel: Check the word wall.

Justin: Ask a friend.

Ben: Try stretching the word out again.

Jordan: Look in our spelling folders.

Adele: Look around the room to see if you can find the word.

Sydney: Use one of the spell checks.

Rachel: Look in a book.

Anna: Use a thesaurus.

Mrs. H-D: Those are all useful suggestions. What is the one thing you don't want to do?

Students: Ask you!

Now the students have a list of independent strategies they can utilize to correct spelling. Hang this chart in the room where the students are able to refer to it.

Mrs. H-D: Adele, we are ready for you now. I'd like you to write the first three words you circled in the column that is labeled Circled Words. (*Adele writes the words. We will only do three words as a group. I can always revisit the lesson, if I see the students need more guidance.*)

Mrs. H-D: Now Adele, I'd like you to look at the chart of spelling strategies and tell me which strategy you're going to try first. (*The word she wrote was* butiful).

Adele: I think I'll ask a friend.

Mrs. H-D: Who will you ask?

Adele: Sydney.

Sydney: I think it is *b-e-u-t-i-f-u-l*.

As Sydney spells the word, Adele writes it under the column that is labeled First Attempt.

Mrs. H-D: You have one more try. Please choose another strategy from the chart.

Adele: I think I will look in a book. I remember the word being part of a title. I think the book is in the fairy tale basket. It is called *Mufaro's Beautiful Daughters*.

Mrs. H-D: Wow, Adele! Great thinking. (*Adele retrieves the book and finds the word.*)

Spelling			
Circled Words	1rst attempt	2nd attempt	Conventional Spelling

Now Adele, please write the word in the second column labeled Second Attempt.

Adele repeats this procedure for the remaining two words. When she finishes, I simply circle the correct word in the appropriate column. If the student did not write the correct spelling, I simply write the word in the column labeled Conventional Spelling. This method is fast and efficient. I encourage students to use two different strategies. That keeps them from writing the word the same way three times. If I see a student spell the word incorrectly the same way three times, I send them back to try again. Also, if that happens more than once, I reteach the lesson.

Mr. H-D: Writers, before I send you off, could someone tell me what you will do next?

Adele: I think we need to fix the spelling in our writing.

Mrs. H-D: You are right! Writers, I would like you to use either a red pen or a colored pencil to correct the spelling. Do not erase your writing. Please write the correct form of the word above the circled word.

When I first started handling spelling in this fashion, I was delighted. I zipped through the forms, and the students were learning on their own. I didn't have to go through their writing, marking their papers. As time went on, students started circling words and using the spelling forms in science or health after completing a writing assignment. The process is ingrained.

Editing for Mechanics

Editing is enjoyable for students when copyediting is taught. After I teach this skill, I notice a marked improvement in the quality of student work across the curriculum. As students learn and practice the symbols, copyediting becomes a natural process. Even young students like copyediting. When I worked as a writing resource teacher, one of the first-grade teachers encountered difficulty with students editing their work. She wanted them to be responsible for capitals at the beginnings of their sentences, punctuation, and spacing. After conferring with the teacher, I decided to teach the students the copyediting symbols that would improve their editing. After a few mini-lessons the students were editing everything, including reading, math, and science assignments! Copyediting is not only a meaningful tool, but is also fun for students.

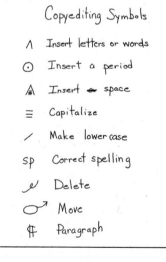

When first establishing a writing workshop, require students to skip lines. Editing and revision are easier for both students and teachers.

I advocate teaching students copyediting for the following reasons: First, it makes students more attentive to the mechanics of writing. Second, when practiced enough, copyediting becomes natural. And third, maybe most important, students enjoy it. When students enjoy an activity, they return to it on their own.

Copyediting Symbols

The following is a simple copyediting sheet. It contains some of the basic symbols I teach second, third, and fourth graders. I give students their own copy to keep in the front of their writing folder. Then I print about ten copies on cardstock and laminate them. These are put in the writing center for reference. Some classroom teachers make a large poster with the editing symbols and hang them for everyone to see.

Copyediting Mini-Lessons

When first introducing the copyediting symbols, I use short sentences or paragraphs from student work. There are a couple of different ways to approach this. Whenever you come across a piece of student work that could be used as a possible teaching lesson, photocopy and file it. My files are full of pieces for revision and editing purposes. I use these pieces to make overheads, or I even run off copies for the class. After a few years, you will have a nice collection of student work to use for mini-lessons. When I find a short piece that would be excellent for editing, I ask the student writer for their permission to make a copy of it to use with other classes. Of course the piece will not have the author's name on it. Most students like their work to be selected for teaching purposes.

	Copyediting Symbols
∧	Insert letters or words
⊙	Insert a period
∧	Insert a space
≡	Capitalize
/	Make lower case
sp	Correct spelling
ℓ	Delete
⟲	Move
¶	Paragraph

I promise I will not use their work in front of them or their classmates. The other way to approach this is by drafting your own sentences and paragraphs from your science, history, or health curriculum.

Lesson 1: Introducing Copyediting Symbols

I determine the number of symbols I introduce at any one time by the following things: grade level, previous writing experience, and instructional need of the students. For instance, some second graders may only be able to handle a few symbols at once, but others may be able to handle all of them. In order to provide differentiation in your classroom you have to look carefully at the needs of your specific classroom population. Many fourth graders have been exposed to the symbols before, so you might conduct a quick review and introduce ones that are not as familiar. My introductory lesson might look like this.

Mrs. H-D: Writers, when real editors edit our work, knowing how to use copyediting symbols helps them to let the writer know the things in their writing that need to be changed. For instance, when I send my writing to the editor, he or she will insert symbols letting me know if I need to paragraph, capitalize, or correct punctuation. (*At this point, I give each student a sheet with the copyediting symbols. On the overhead, I put a few sentences, or paragraphs that need editing, and give each student a copy for their own practice.*) Learning to copyedit will help you find the errors that need correcting before you send your work out to the public. Let's look at the first symbol. You will see three little lines under the name jasmine. Can anyone tell me why the *j* has three little lines under it?

> Punctuation Takes a Vacation *by Robin Pulver* is an excellent book to share with students. This book not only includes some basic punctuation rules, but also teaches students the results of not including punctuation in their writing. It is well crafted and lots of fun for students.

Jasmine: The *j* has that symbol for two reasons. One is because Jasmine is the first word of the sentence. And the other is because Jasmine is a proper noun. It needs to be capitalized.

Mrs. H-D: You are correct. Now writers please look through the practice writing I provided you with. Please put three little lines under anything that is not capitalized and needs to be capitalized.

Continue the lesson above with as many symbols as you feel your students are able to handle.

As a follow-up activity, I often have students copyedit several versions of the same sentence using the symbols we've learned. This particular sentence (shown on page 45) was from student work. I asked permission to use this sentence for a teaching lesson. Save examples of student work for this. Look for sentences you can write in different ways for students to practice using copyediting symbols. I took the following sentence from Brenna's piece about her grandmother. Give each student a copy and make one overhead. Have students correct their own copy. Then put a copy on the overhead and ask students to come up and insert the correct symbols. The other students check or correct their own copy.

Grandma lost her coffee mug
grandma lost her coffe mug.
Grandma lost her coffeemug.
Grandma lost her coffee mug.

Lesson 2: Copyedit Student Work

Have students copyedit the same piece of student work. For this lesson, either pull from your student work file or ask a student from your present class for permission to use their piece. Caution! Make sure the student understands their work will be used for editing; their classmates will be looking for mistakes. Copy the piece on a transparency and make individual copies for the rest of the class. Allow a few minutes for students to copyedit the student work, using either a pen or colored pencil. Then call the student writer to the overhead and display the piece. Ask the student writer to read it aloud, pausing after each sentence to look for errors and correct them with copyediting symbols.

forever . . .
forever I will love my mom and dad, also my teacher.
I will care about my friends forever.
I will care about my learning (Ireaning) forever.
I will love my kitten forever.

Student ... grade 2

Lesson 3: Interactive Editing

This lesson is my favorite. It is called an interactive edit. You will need markers and a large chart with a story, poem, or letter like the one at right. When you write the piece, make common errors in it. Display the text, read it through once, and then have students come forward one at a time and copyedit and correct a mistake. Keep it moving. Students love to do this and they are very good at finding the teacher's mistakes. The first time I did this with second graders one little guy raised his hand and said, "This is so much fun. You should make these up all the time so we can practice editing." My reply was "Why would I do that? All you have to do is find one of your pieces of writing in your folder that needs editing and you can do the same thing." He smiled and told me he had never thought of that.

As Cute as a Button
you should meet my dog lucy.
she is funny. Toilet paper is here.
favorite thing. she jumps up up, grabs the toilet papee, and runs through the hose Mr. dove gets made at her and tells her go to bed. then lucy whines and looks at him with her big, brown eyes. eyes. I just smele becuz i think she as cut as a button

Lesson 4: Morning Editing Practice

I believe students should be engaged in learning from the time they arrive at school until they leave. As soon as my students walk through the door, they know to check out the large whiteboard near the meeting area. (A chalkboard or large sheet of paper would work just as well.) Every morning on that board there is an activity that requires a written response. Students are required to respond on the board at least three times a week; on other days, they may choose to visit the library, read, or set daily goals for accomplishing tasks.

After announcements, we gather around and students read their responses. Now when we are focusing on the editing process students will edit their work if it isn't written correctly. I find it amazing how quickly they catch their own mistakes. I usually don't have to prompt them; students support each other in collaborative ways by respectfully reminding each other what needs to be edited.

Editing in Writing Workshop

During writing workshop the editing process follows revision and comes before publishing. Of course, some students edit every time they reread, and this is fine. They should also do a final edit before publishing. When working in my own classroom, or while consulting, I use the following procedure. First, students take an editing checklist, such as the one shown above. After they have edited for spelling using the spelling sheet described on page 42, they check off the spelling box and continue through the checklist.

The next step is for the writer to meet with a co-editor, another student in the class. The co-editor and the writer reread the piece together. The co-editor's responsibility is to make sure that the writer has sufficiently edited the piece. Then the co-editor checks off the appropriate boxes and signs his or her name. The writer may then submit the piece to the final editor, the teacher. As final editor, I do not require every mistake to be corrected, but I must see that there has

Name:_____ Editing Checklist				
Date:_____ Title:_____				
Check for:	Editor	Co-Editor	Final Editor	Comments or Suggestions
Spelling — Spelling errors Circled and corrected				
Capitals — Beginning of sentences Proper Nouns				
Punctuation . ? !				
Commas — Where needed				
Quotations — To show where dialogue begins and ends				
Signatures				

Try not to overwhelm students by asking them to edit for too many things. For example, you may want second graders to work on spelling. Once they have mastered spelling, you may want to introduce capitalization and punctuation. This checklist serves as a guideline. I encourage each teacher to design his or her own checklists to meet the needs of students.

been ample effort on the part of the writer to complete the editing process. If the writer's piece is revised and edited, as final editor I check and sign off and send it to our publishing center. If the piece needs more work, I give it back to the writer. At that point, the writer decides if he or she will revise or edit again. If not, the piece will not be published. If students understand how the process works, most are willing to put forth the effort to have their piece published.

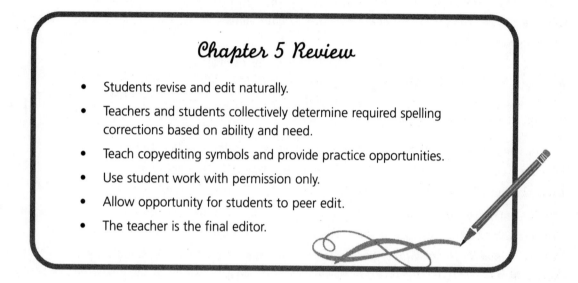

Chapter 5 Review

- Students revise and edit naturally.
- Teachers and students collectively determine required spelling corrections based on ability and need.
- Teach copyediting symbols and provide practice opportunities.
- Use student work with permission only.
- Allow opportunity for students to peer edit.
- The teacher is the final editor.

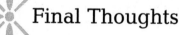

Final Thoughts

Revision and editing are key steps in the writing process, yet too often writers approach them warily. By fostering a playful attitude and focusing on the purpose of these steps— to make meaning clearer for the reader—you can help transform students' attitudes. With lots of modeling and direct instruction of specific strategies, along with plenty of time to practice and share, students will begin to appreciate the power of revision and eagerly revise and edit their work.

Bibliography

Children's Books Cited

Bryant, Jill and Catherine Heard. *Making Shadow Puppets*. Toronto, Canada: Kids Can Press, 2002.

Carlson, Nancy. *I Like Me!* New York: Viking Penguin, Inc., 1988.

Coles, Robert. *The Story of Ruby Bridges*. New York: Scholastic, 1995.

dePaola, Tomie. *The Popcorn Book*. New York: Holiday House, 1984.

Florian, Douglas. *Winter Eyes*. New York: Greenwillow, 1999.

French, Fiona. *Snow White in New York*. Oxford: Oxford University Press, 1986.

Ketteman, Helen. *I Remember Papa*. New York: Dial Books, 1998.

Lollis, Sylvia and Joyce W. Hogan. *Should We Have Pets? A Persuasive Text*. New York: Mondo Publishing, 2002.

Martin, Jacqueline Briggs. *Snowflake Bentley*. Boston: Houghton Mifflin, 1998.

Meadows, Graham. *Arctic Foxes and Red Foxes*. Carlsbad, CA: Dominie Press, 2002.

Nelson, Robin. *From Wax to Crayon*. Minneapolis, MN: Lerner Publications, 2003.

O'Neill, Mary. *Hailstone and Halibut Bones*. Garden City, New York: Doubleday and Company, Inc., 1961.

Paulsen, Gary. *Canoe Days*. New York: Bantam Doubleday Dell Publishing Group, Inc., 1999.

Poulton, Kimberly. *Hello Willow*. North Kingston, RI: Moon Mountain Publishing, 2000.

Pringle, Lawrence. *Bats! Strange and Wonderful*. Honesdale, PA: Boyds Mills Press, 2000.

Pulver, Robin. *Punctuation Takes a Vacation*. New York: Scholastic, 2003.

Rylant, Cynthia. *Let's Go Home*. New York: Simon & Schuster Books for Young Readers, 2002.

Rylant, Cynthia. *Mr. Putter and Tabby Pour the Tea*. New York: Scholastic, 1994.

Rylant, Cynthia. *Night in the Country*. New York: Simon & Schuster, 1986.

Rylant, Cynthia. *Scarecrow*. San Diego: Voyager Books Harcourt, Inc., 2001.

Rylant, Cynthia. *The Whales*. New York: Scholastic, 1996.

Rylant, Cynthia. *When I Was Young in the Mountains*. New York: Dutton, 1982.

Shields, Carol Diggory. *Lucky Pennies and Hot Chocolate*. New York: Dutton Children's Books, 2000.

Steptoe, John. *Mufaro's Beautiful Daughters: An African Tale*. New York: Lothrop, Lee & Shepard, 1987.

Wood, Audrey. *The Napping House*. San Diego: Harcourt Brace Jovanovich, Publishers, 1984.

Wood, Audrey. *The Red Racer*. New York: Simon & Schuster Books for Young Readers, 1996.

Zolotow, Charlotte. *My Friend John*. New York: Random House Children's Book, 2000.

Zolotow, Charlotte. *The Seashore Book*. HarperCollinsPublishers, 1992.

Professional Books Cited

Fletcher, Ralph. *A Writer's Notebook*. New York: HarperCollins, 1996.

Heard, Georgia. *The Revision Toolbox*. Portsmouth, NH: Heinemann, 2002.

Routman, Regie. *Conversations*. Portsmouth, NH: Heinemann, 2000.

Ray, Katie Wood. *What You Know by Heart*. Portsmouth, NH: Heinemann, 2002.

Periodicals

Horn Book